Dear Dreamland

Dear Dreamland
Markham Johnson

LITERARY PRESS
LAMAR UNIVERSITY

Copyright © Lamar University Literary Press 2022
All rights reserved

ISBN: 978-0-692-42501-5
Library of Congress Control Number: 2022939311

Cover Design: Public Domain

Lamar University Literary Press
Beaumont, Texas

For my grandmothers who told me their stories.

And so, for my sake, I bring them back.

B. H. Fairchild

Recent Poetry from Lamar University Literary Press

Bobby Aldridge, *An Affair of the Stilled Heart*
Walter Bargen, *My Other Mother's Red Mercedes*
Charles Behlen, *Failing Heaven*
Jerry Bradley, *Collapsing into Possibility*
Mark Busby, *Through Our Times*
Julie Chappell, *Mad Habits of a Life*
Stan Crawford, *Resisting Gravity*
Glover Davis, *My Cap of Darkness*
William Virgil Davis, *The Bones Poems*
Jeffrey DeLotto, *Voices Writ in Sand*
Chris Ellery, *Elder Tree*
Dede Fox, *On Wings of Silence*
Alan Gann, *That's Entertainment*
Larry Griffin, *Cedar Plums*
Michelle Hartman, *Irony and Irrelevance*
Katherine Hoerth, *Goddess Wears Cowboy Boots*
Michael Jennings, *Crossings: A Record of Travel*
Gretchen Johnson, *A Trip Through Downer, Minnesota*
Ulf Kirchdorfer, *Hamlet in Exhile*
Jim McGarrah, *A Balancing Act*
J. Pittman McGehee, *Nod of Knowing*
Erin Murphy, *Ancilla*
John Milkereit, *Drive the World in a Taxicab*
Laurence Musgrove, *Bluebonnet Sutras*
Benjamin Myers, *Black Sunday*
Janice Northerns, *Some Electric Hum*
Godspower Oboido, *Wandering Feet on Pebbled Shores*
Carol Coffee Reposa, *Underground Musicians*
Jan Seale, *Particulars*
Steven Schroeder, *the moon, not the finger, pointing*
Glen Sorestad, *Hazards of Eden*
Vincent Spina, *The Sumptuous Hills of Gulfport*
W.K. Stratton, *Betrayal Creek*
Wally Swist, *Invocation*
Ken Waldman, *Sports Page*
Loretta Diane Walker, *Ode to My Mother's Voice*
Dan Williams, *Past Purgatory, a Distant Paradise*
Jonas Zdanys, *Three White Horses*

For information on these and other Lamar University Literary Press books go to www.Lamar.edu/literarypress

Acknowledgements

I am grateful to the editors of the following publications who have published some of the poems in this collection:

Nimrod
Bull Buffalo and Indian Paintbrush (The Poetry of Oklahoma)
Coal Hill Review
Comstock Review
Conestoga Zen
Consequence Magazine
English Journal
Greenwood One Hundred published by The Black Wall Street Times
This Land
The Ekphrastic Review
Nine Mile Magazine
San Pedro River Review
Sport Literate

Gratitude

Roger Weingarten provided invaluable help as I worked through this manuscript, as he has with my writing since I was an MFA student when Roger directed the program at Vermont College.

Special thanks to Eder Williams McKnight, Persis Karim, Tom Tomshany, Jane Beckwith, Quraysh Ali Lansana, Michael Mason, Greg Carey, and the late Jack Myers for their great support. I am also very grateful to two thousand Holland Hall students who have written and talked poetry with me over the years.

My deepest thanks to my wife Dawn and my friend Chris Seid who have been telling me the hard truth all my adult life.

CONTENTS

Before We Were Men

- 14 Booker T. Washington High School Graduation—Tulsa, Oklahoma
- 16 Tennis Whites
- 17 Blown Futures in Royce Carter's Orange VW Bug
- 18 Army Physical at Ft. Sill
- 19 Saints Save Me
- 21 Last Paperboys in Oklahoma Carry the News
- 22 Coach Green in The Bardo
- 24 Taken
- 26 Hitching a Ride to the Rapture
- 27 Trouble Light, September 15, 1963
- 28 Longhorn
- 29 Lesser Laws of Gravity
- 30 Pony Up—Last Pit Pony in Oklahoma
- 31 We Ride Trouble
- 32 Twister
- 33 Bangs!
- 35 Summer's Discordant Joy
- 37 This Hand
- 38 Kenny Bright Loads Spencer
- 40 Dead, Lonnie Wins
- 41 Late Shift on the Loading Dock
- 42 Before We Were Men
- 45 Ghost Fish

Postcards from a Massacre

- 48 Grandma Ruth, Last Day of School, 1921
- 50 Go Down Moses
- 51 Aaron Carter, No Man's Land
- 53 A.J. Smitherman, Death of the *Tulsa Star*
- 54 Postcard Sonnets from a Massacre
- 66 The Way to Zion

This Time You're Going to Win

68	Father with Railroad Trestle, 1947
70	Ghost of Hank Williams at Cain's Ballroom, 1954
72	The Sex Pistols at Cain's, 1978
73	Last Texas Playboys at Cain's , 1984
74	Taxi Dancer—Cain's Dance Academy, 1932
75	Hank's Back, 1961
76	Ghost
77	At the Red Formica Table Where We Forget
79	Running the Murder of Pigs Marathon
81	At the Track Waiting for Jesus
83	Advent with Audubon
84	The Deluge
85	Honest to God
87	Stigmata
88	Eschatology
89	Noodling the Void
90	Dante Gabriel Rossetti's *Beata Beatrix*
91	John Everett Millais' *Ophelia*
93	Mother at Seventeen
94	Pennies
95	Oklahoma Odyssey
97	Falling
99	Florence Learns to Fly

Notes

One of the worst race massacres in the history of the United States occurred in Tulsa, Oklahoma in 1921. Much of the photographic evidence we have of the Tulsa Race Massacre comes from postcards that were printed and distributed by the KKK and other members of the white mob that torched Greenwood, the prosperous black district of Tulsa.

"Grandma Ruth, Last Day of School"
When she was a high school student, my grandmother witnessed a wagonload of bodies being hauled away to a mass grave in Oaklawn Cemetery. In 1921 the Dreamland Theater presented nationally prominent African-American performers.

"A.J. Smitherman: Death of the *Tulsa Star*"
The Tulsa Star was one of two newspapers that served Greenwood. Its owner and publisher, A.J. Smitherman, was a community leader who fought to end lynchings. Though he tried to stop the white mob during the Tulsa Race Massacre, he was indicted for inciting the riot and fled Tulsa.

"Postcard Sonnets from a Massacre"
When Dick Rowland, a young black man, was arrested after he stumbled and fell against a white elevator operator, Sarah Page, the mob that tried to lynch him was stopped by residents of Greenwood including black WW1 veterans. Frustrated, the mob stormed into Greenwood and burned it to the ground. At the time, Tulsa with its meteoric growth was known as the Magic City. Postcards distributed after Greenwood was destroyed showed burning buildings, dead bodies in the streets, and survivors being marched to internment camps. In this series of poems about the Tulsa Race Massacre, I used sonnets, a form of poetry that might fit on a postcard.

Before We Were Men

Booker T. Washington High School Graduation—Tulsa, Oklahoma

Half a century ago, last day of school, a white mob
torched Dreamland, Brown's Cafe, Madam C.J.

Walker's Beauty Parlor, and every church in Greenwood.
At Booker T. Washington, prom banners flapping

like busted wings, they turned away. Tonight,
in this theater, where some say Tulsa Race Massacre

dead were fed to basement boiler flames, I am one
of seven, first white graduates, one of 257

gowned in black. Tonight, my friends and I are little more
human than clay, even Royce Carter quoting

Malcolm X. *I'm for truth no matter who tells it.
I'm for justice no matter who for.* He's searching

the crowd for Moses. His father, as a child,
cloaked in cattails, was saved from torch lit KKK.

When I turn to look where Royce waves, I see Grandpa
Jake rise from his chair in the back row. Angry,

he wants to leave. Years before, as I waited in line
for baseball autographs, Grandpa raised me

to those derrickman shoulders so I could reach
Satchel Page. Later, gowned in white, he blazed

in the light of two crucified railroad ties on a hill
over Greenwood. *If you don't stand for something,*

you'll fall for anything, Royce chants, as Grandpa paces
the aisle, bumping folding chairs, the way

he drives, flanks of his Roadmaster pocked
with small tragedies. Is that walnut sized tumor

already crowding his brain? Does his world catch
and turn over like the Buick's balky starter? Let's say,

I remember how he held me, tiny, in those broken
driller's mitts. Let's say, I still love though I can't forgive.

Let's say, I hear his voice going blind.

Tennis Whites

Royce hates tennis, but loves to smack
pale suburban boys with fuzzy yellow balls.

Get away from my net, he mouths
as our opponents rub red welts. He doesn't

look back when I laugh, but it's 1972,
and I'm the only white kid playing tennis

for Booker T. Washington High. *Serve,
Johnson,* he nods, linebacker hands wringing

steel racket. At singles, we fail: ground
strokes, like purple martins chase

mayflies, passing shots clang off posts
one court over. Even in doubles,

Royce and I must win points quickly,
losing long rallies to teams dressed in IZOD.

My serve is flat and hard, peeling paint
from worn cement, so the return wobbles

across the net. *Yes,* Royce grins,
while the skinny boy on the other side swears

fidelity to the goddess of segregated
schools, unsure which body part to protect.

He would flee, but his father in the bleachers
leans in as my doubles partner raises

his racket to invoke centuries of revenge.
Royce, I'm still playing on your side.

Blown Futures in Royce Carter's Orange VW Bug

Someone, in joy or pain, had jammed a hard left heel
into the speaker, so the radio plays

Bridge Over Troubled Water reprised by Elmer Fudd,
while we wait to discover who will be taken.

Jacob, I believe, smelling of weed and Mogen David.
Maybe Barry who at 5'4" has faith the army

sergeant will laugh and ship him home. Not
Royce who stares down the fuzzed radio

like Uri Geller at a banquet of spoons.
Finally, May 17, his birthday, is called: *Number 135*.

You're out, we scream, toasting with grape Nehi
a renewed future of football and a scholarship to Penn.

The others begin to scoot out the back, draft lottery
prayers answered, but Royce waits with me

for a final five hundred heartbeats, this minor eternity,
until my number, 25, is revealed. He leans over,

whispers behind his hand, the way we devise
tennis doubles strategy. *Dude, you'll die in Vietnam.*

Army Physical at Ft. Sill

Seven hours from Tulsa to the barracks
where Geronimo fell drunk
from his horse and died, the Army
camo bus collects young men
from Greyhound stations: Sparks
to Mustang to Pumpkin Center.
Sleepless from adrenaline
and dexedrine, I move seat
to seat, sharing stories as we cruise
silent Oklahoma blacktop. Someone
has to remember I promise
roadkill armadillo and white
tailed deer. At eighteen, I can redeem
this loneliness, I believe, this first
time I know I will write. About
these lapsed teenage boys—
I can say they are black,
white, Apache, from Okarche, Beggs,
Bugtussle—who, weeks after
high school graduation, fall in love
with small town girls or boys, while
uncles and cousins are boxed
and tagged, in An Loc and Quang Tri,
return to sender. When I ask
What will you do now? no one
has an answer. Oh
God of Oklahoma children, almost
innocent, who might still
hitch a long haul north. *Canada,*
I say, *I know someone,*
but they've learned to lean
into hard packed futures and fall
for a few hours sleep.

Saints Save Me

Rising from highway fog, the first hitchhiker I've seen
in thirty years—one hand slipped behind

his back, prison guard tower half a mile south.
Grandma would have picked him up. At my age,

now, she collected walleyed hobos, women
dragging dingy children through moonlight, then

waved them back to Route 66 after chicken fried
steak and sweet potato pie at Goldy's.

Once, after collecting me from school, Grandma drove
her friend Peace Pilgrim back to the interstate to continue

a fifth cross country ramble. *What will he do
when he's drafted?* Peace leaned over the front seat

to inspect my ponytail, wondering if I was worth
saving. I hadn't read Ghandi or Krishnamurti

or any prophets Grandma assigned, but
at seventeen, I was sure I could think for myself.

All I knew of bodhisattvas, tzadikim were faux stained
glass saints eyeballing me through hour-long

sermons, faces puckered as if just waking to Great
Aunt Carol farting in the pew beside me. *I don't believe*

in Vietnam, I said, recalling how
Cody Hightower's older brother drilled me

with a pellet gun in the neck. Peace
shook her long white hair, turned away, *As good*

as dead, while Grandma flapped an arm
over the seat, trying to dispel my thick teenage

stupidity. *You don't believe in war, period,* Grandma
tore each word from the next, as if

they might escape my leaky brain. Fifty years
later, I've found my final draft board notice: grim

white men forgave my dumb song lyrics,
sentimental prose, and sent me back to school.

Peace, I mutter sweeping leaves from Grandma's
grave, hoping the old gals would still be proud.

The Last Paperboys in Oklahoma Carry the News

Five a.m. bundles litter the highway
patrol station front porch where Southside
paperboys pop Lucifer
matches on thumbnails and wrap *Tulsa
Worlds* with green rubber bands.
This day, Jackson Harlow spits Red Man
on a cruiser. This day, Stevie Logan, who never
busted a porch milk bottle and might
have hurled six or seven seasons
of minor league ball, kick
starts the pop machine for a lifetime
of lost dimes and quarters. What if
we'd just walked away with all
the cokes we could carry? What if
the night let us drift and wake late
on a Saturday to another summer of teenage
afternoons? What if Jackson and Stevie
hadn't peddled their Schwinns into false
dawn, cutting through a rain culvert
under Highway 44 as an envoy
of cicadas chanted a Greek
chorus of regret? What if fifty years
later I didn't carry the blank
slate of their passing or wake to the shape
note hymn of a thousand starlings
calling me to believe again.

Coach Green in The Bardo
for Ron Wallace

His team flailing at change-ups rooting
like nightcrawlers through red clay,
Coach Green yells *You can't hit
what you can't see,* while in wood-rot
stands, grandfathers dig dreams
of athletic legacy loose
from the roots. *Just, a dying quail,*
he begs, as back to the dugout I drag
my Louisville Slugger and tear off
the plastic helmet Arnie Green drilled
with a hanging slider when I dropped
below the Mendoza line. *Blood
makes the grass grow.* Half-deaf, I heard
nothing until he waved his magic
clipboard over our heads, chanting *Any
of you can be the next Mickey Mantle.*
Even me, Coach? I asked. Oh
minor gods of little league, oh
broken heartwood of dugout
pine, some nights I wake at three a.m.
with gouts of failure pumping
through my cerebellum, watch him
lean over the seat because only
girls need eyes to drive, point
his unfiltered Camel, and spit
Not you, Johnson. This morning, when
my retriever claims another
baseball from the woods, I hear a groan
rise from the third base
coaches box in the Bardo and Arnie
Green mouthing *It was right
in your wheelhouse,* while some
poor fifth grader fists another so foul
it's only fair for dogs and doesn't
even run it out, though Coach's screaming
and teammates up and down
the bench smell doom wafting

from the green porta potty by the snack
shack and don't even try
to bring that one back from the bog.
But not Ajax, who breaks
from the woods and races
past third, with the rain blackened
ball in his jaws, and after
bearing it gently through our long
walk, trots back to the infield
grass where some cosmic residue
of atomized Arnie Green's mesmerized
to watch him *tear the cover off the ball.*

Taken

Weeks after Pastor Bob preaches apocalypse,
my cousins and I await a lonely Chevy or Ford,

no hands palming the steering wheel. While
in the driveway, my unsaved uncle, buried

in entropy and resurrection—a blown head gasket,
oil blackening the breadth of a Dodge slant six—slides

new O rings into the broken Dart
like the pastor parking the Eucharist on Molly Flynn's

pink tongue. Yes, we were endowed
with imagination and very little sense, but

for years Matt, Chris, and I were stuffed
in the rear of Grandma's Wagonmaster, backwards,

atoms of empty space squashed between flailing
arms and legs, our starter kit brains firing

random questions: *Will God fix Chuckie
Cunningham's blown plugs and points? Who'll feed*

*Harry the hamster when Jesus
calls us home?* Years later, hitching from Florida

Panhandle to Oklahoma, where my parents'
marriage flapped like cheap retread, I flagged

a ride—a Cadillac DeVille huffing gray
clouds of high test into the still

to be born morning, dragged my fingers down
those side panels, sleek as a quarter

horse, to a yawning trunk and bumper sticker—
In Case of Rapture, This Vehicle Will Be

Unmanned, and recalled the weeks I'd waited for
a driverless sedan to bang the curb and settle

on our lawn. Where were my cousins now?
I prayed they were locked in a clutch

of girlfriends, binding them to good red dirt, not
waiting to be claimed. I watched gasoline vapor

vanish in the stunned gasp of first light,
felt the V-8 purr, and tossed my pack in.

Hitching a Ride to the Rapture

Lonely and waiting for God to take him
in his '72 DeVille, with silvered
flanks, Carl wanted her gentled
when he disappeared, eased

to the side of the road, not flopping
like a dying trout in a ditch
and begged me to sleep light,
so, if he were called, I could snag

the wheel. *Even Oklahoma's on the way,*
he said, his voice like the AM
radio station outside Biloxi,
where we swam in the cosmic

slop of ocean, a crescent moon riding
ripples on blood warm water. Back
on the road, I startled to find him,
head rolled up, headlights off, hands

pressed together, as if preparing
to ascend through Detroit steel. *Just
practicing,* he said and pointed to a Paradise,
Texas highway sign, 213 miles.

Now, or a billion miles from now,
I imagine Carl riding the coda of one last
turnpike, stars so close they seem
the hoodliner of some celestial machine.

He pulls off the road, nighthawks soaring
through headlights, stretching
hands toward the moon, hoping
he too will learn to fly.

Trouble Light, September 15, 1963

Under the raised hood of a Plymouth,
wheels gone, oil striping the driveway,

in white framed Polaroid memory
my uncle leans into bare bulbed

light that spills at dusk over this wreck
that just wants to play dead. In

the backyard, the cousins and I slash
tennis balls with warped

golf clubs scavenged from grandma's
shed: mashie, niblick, cleek, names

like 60s side dishes steaming
on the supper table. We're trying

to clear the privacy fence, but gray
fuzzless balls volley back hard enough

to tear off a face. At twilight the stir
of oak leaves stills like small feet gone

to ground. In the darkness that rises
from the lawn, June bugs bash

bone hard heads on the 60 watt
bulb, then fall into the Valiant's

torn engine. No trouble here,
just hazed TV light from a window

where Walter Cronkite can barely say
In Birmingham, four little girls—

Longhorn

In backyard wiffle ball doubleheaders, we claimed
names of favorite players. My cousins: Mays

and Marichal. Mine: Gibson and Brock. *But they're negroes*,
said Chuckie. Sliders and Matt's yellow hammer

curve dived beneath Chuckie's bat, until, in the fermented
anthem of bees drunk on honeysuckle, he caught

one and drove that ball across the road to settle
behind chain link where a Texas Longhorn raised

his head. Losers had to reclaim home runs
from the ditch, but for this gone ball we gathered

twelve feet above the pond. Once we'd hauled
an alligator snapper from the muck and knew

a first step in the meadow would raise a cicada rant
to summon the lord of the prairie. Halfway

between azure joy and green despair, I froze,
Keds scraping concrete wall, while Matt dropped

in quackgrass. We saw yellow-eyed death stir
from kicking a trench in ragged earth. *Yea,*

though I walk through the valley, Chuckie
whispered as horns turned, deadly beacons

that swept the pasture. Did we believe our prayers
would bear him home? Fifty years later

I'm left to dream that terror, to tell the story:
some nights my fingers seek his, to drag Matt clear.

Lesser Laws of Gravity

We loved the nothing it held: emptiness
my sister and I scooped out, cool air surging
up the tin chute from Grandmother's basement
miles below. After watching her vanish

piles of pillowcases and dirty sheets,
we dropped tomatoes and fresh eggs, witness
to the moment they disappeared. Almost
a miracle until they splattered on

concrete floor. When we learned to center
the basket halfway in-between mangle
and furnace, we found them whole, again, neck
deep in moist laundry, nesting in silence,

and knew we too could channel God's wonder
that what we claimed, then lost, might be restored.

Pony Up - Last Pit Pony in Oklahoma

Suzie's lucky, says Grandma, who claimed her cheap
at the Claremore Rodeo, because no fool would bid

on a Shetland with fourteen years of mean staked
to her heart. The last pit pony in Oklahoma, dredged

from the mines, almost blind from years dragging wagon-loads
of zinc and lead through the dark. Grandma understood—

when you're raised up hard and half wild, kindness
has to force a channel under the skin. Trailered to Spunky

Creek Farm, Dad pulls the pins, drops the gate,
to loose Suzie in the pasture where she'll grow tough

and fat on acorns and hay. Thirteen that summer, slugging
dirt clods and racing chickens around

the barn, we catch her napping and cull Suzie
from big thoroughbred studs. Cousin Chris climbs

on, legs stuck straight out, kicking sneakers in the air, because
he can't reach her ribs, then falls hard. Suzie knows all

the low branched oaks and sycamores she can just squeeze
under and the blackberry patch, thick and full

of thorns. This pony that never loved me watches
as I slide one leg over her back. Knees hugged to heaving

sides, I tuck my head tight to her neck, cool
as a grave, try to be brave, and know I'll fail.

But at thirteen you jump aboard, get scraped
off and in an Oklahoma summer's red dust, rise again.

We Ride Trouble

Furrows, we dream true each night, shimmer
like highway dashes in heat
off Route 66 as the cousins and I ride
Grandma's Farmall tractor, carving
rows through fallow acres by dead
reckoning. As Matt drives,
Chris and I scatter seed corn
and cling to the spring
seat, praying we'll not be ground
beneath iron wheels before we sell
our cash crop to high school
girls parked on blacktop who might
desire more than Oklahoma
Xtra Sweet. As we turn the red
beast beside the ditch, some god-swarm
of mud daubers rouses from steep
banks and slaps us back
to reality. Chris and I leap free, but Matt
remains, jamming the brake pedal
lock too late, the tractor
submarining in Spunky Creek. After
that, we hoe a hundred red clay rows
by hand. Though we'll ride trouble
together, again, that day we struggle
home through blistered
sunlight. Peeling shoulders leaned
close for support, we wade
the last pasture with flint
arrowhead offerings, miniature
gravestones perched on Grandma's yellow
window ledge, then skedaddle
to the pump house behind Wolf
Robe's Trading Post, where in cool adobe
silence, she won't find us until nightfall.

Twister

In Oklahoma, the hand of God trolls corn
cribs and trailer parks the afternoon

my little brother flapping his arms, heart
skidding under flannel, yells *Twister,*

and we follow to the porch where a black
fist from an ebony cloud punches

holes in a house a mile away. Cicada wings
grow drunk as stone; all the front lawn

squirrels tuck their tails, pointing
down the street where the neighborhood pool's

being sucked dry. Parcels of privacy
fence sizzle past dogs and barbecues levitating

while Mr. Conroy's Chris Craft circles,
then splits like a giant pinata against our post

oak. In a plague of deck chairs we turn
together and flee for the bathtub to pray

to the gods of seamless plumbing. When
our broken world stills, will I remember

the guiding principle of Brothers Grimm
tales? The humble youngest son saves

his family from a double ration of stone
cold misery, one beaten heart at a time.

Bangs!

That summer, they were mostly hyphens—
my mom and her pals. Killing time

at the kitchen table over cocktails and menthol
lights, they'd slipped the fundamental

grammar of holding families together, period.
Once I returned from roofing a house to find Z

alone, doodling, while the others circled discount
racks for knock-off Givenchy

and Yves Saint Laurent. She caught me
staring and raised a postcard, smeared

with an ellipsis of inked exclamation
marks. Bangs, she called them, a term Scott

Fitzgerald whispered when he kissed her,
only 14, at a New Year's party. Maybe

she held my hand longer than intended,
then swiped away four conjoined red

commas on my cheek with one lip
moistened finger. When she slipped

a book into my palm, I tucked it under
my pillow to read after I'd returned

from Molly, Lisa, or Angeline. Two
days later, Z diagrammed a flat line

of pills, a white wordless resolution. God
damn it, Z. At seventeen, we are silly half-made

creatures, with only a little goodness
to conceal. All it took to change my life

was a smear of kindness, a few
Rorschach stains on the table, and death's

pale light dragged across the room.
Sometimes at 3 a.m. I slide *Gatsby*

off the nightstand, untuck the postcard,
trace the bangs falling off the edge,

and remember a night when the cousins
and I stole Buds from the fridge, then watched you

swing to Nat Cole in the living room with
your husband or someone else's, barefoot,

with perfect little steps, then a twirl. Sometimes
we are less substantial than air.

Summer's Discordant Joy

Wood chipper, power mower, mockingbird—a thousand
dissonant voices flown with the sun. Still the Avery twins

are spouting gladness through neighborhood twilight:
someone squeals, a car door slams, laughter vaults

the privacy fence. In the shadow of the neighbor's disabled
tree fort, a chorus line of tree frogs serenades

late rain. But when a barn owl sails through,
even the grass goes dumb. He's hunting, wing

feathers gentle cooling air—pure silence
in the combustion of a summer suburban night.

Somewhere, Harvey Hanson still spit-sprays *Rock
of Ages, Shall We Gather at the River*, tone deaf,

praising his Lord. Every choir night of my sixteenth
summer, we, teenage basses in the back row, poked fingers

in our offended ears— each blast from Harvey a small
cowpie of contempt for music we'd almost come to love

while passing whole notes to Julie
Underwood and Molly Flynn, sopranoing

in the front. Wednesdays we prayed rain-slicked
streets would pothole Harvey—tires punched

flat, holes bored in his deflated pride. Tonight
when the Avery twins are gone, and the sonic

grace note in our backyard has sailed on, fireflies
scale the major staff of the picket fence, a possum

family slides across a neighbor's
roof, and the old raccoon dragging one paw waits

to claim cat food spilled on the stoop.
The week Harvey was clipped, singing great choral gouts

through downtown streets, we were sure, somehow,
we'd conducted that 5:15 bus cutting the corner

at 6th and Boston, bearing down hard on such
discordant joy. For weeks of Sunday mornings,

both legs cast in plaster, he leaned his red
flat top back to watch us stand in the choir loft—altos

dragging columns of Sunday reverence into aging
lungs, the prettiest young sopranos in Tulsa

sliding glissandos into our breast pockets, while we three
teenage basses, our unfinished voices

now exposed, mouthed the words, silent as night
owls searching out the innocent, the lame.

This Hand

Moan of crickets in the weeds. Even the barred owl's
ghost cries carry no news as my old dog fades
into bushes by the fence, raising his head to sniff cosmic

residue drifting through trees where a last possum
or fox passed not long ago. Tonight, I imagine every
poet in the world on a back porch, pen in hand,

waiting for the right words to slide over Cross Burning
Hill, the way a class 4 tornado unzipped half
the roofs in our neighborhood. I spent that summer

banging penny nails into vinyl sheets above
bedrooms, kitchens, living rooms aching
to be restored. Months later, I sat half lotus

on the floor of Jerusalem's Dome of the Rock.
No one spoke. No one watched as I slid one arm
into a tunnel of fist-sized darkness, trusting

my fingers to find the foundation stone—where
Mohammad ascended on winged Buraq, where
Abraham, Moses, and Jesus waved him home. That summer

everything seemed torn open. That summer this blind
hand fingered the cold, granite face
of Zion, searched for hoofprints, for footprints

then pulled free, slipping the latticed hole, empty,
scented of saffron some pilgrim had spilled. That summer,
this hand tasted dust from God's shoes.

Kenny Bright Loads Spencer

Three years after the fall of Saigon, Kenny Bright
chokes the breath from augurs, drive shafts,

gripping tight as a band saw before letting go.
Each night he loads Spencer, worst job

on the dock. An eight hour fusillade of freight jamming
the belt in front of his truck, Kenny breaks

from semi-trailer murk, grabs an arm load of boxes,
and returns, framing a foxhole from car seats,

windshields, console TVs bound for Storm Lake
and Marathon. *Dude's got demons,*

says Babo who knows the story—PFC Bright,
night blind, leaps from a Huey Cobra into

nothing, rice paddies twenty feet below.
After seven hours of tracer rounds, Viet Cong keening

in the dark, the helicopter crew pulls the teenage
marine clear of mud and whatever remains

of men, not men. At lunch break, I play pitch
for quarter pots with Babo and Lurch,

while Kenny, on the cracked lip of a formica chair,
chases the butt end of one unlucky day

with the next. Half past midnight,
the last freight loaded, the Spencer driver drags

the max weight trailer clear of the dock,
while Kenny stares into a parking lot, where a single

blighted elm coned in streetlight bears
hundreds of monarchs fanning wings in the cooling

night. I'd like to say I don't know the rest.
I returned to school, but not before Kenny stepped

off the dock into a smear of fog, tinted
green from the all-night soybean processing plant,

crossed the abandoned railroad spur, then just
kept walking, south to the river. Oh, my broken

country, for Kenny Bright there is no polished
granite wall our fingers might trace. Anyone

listening would have believed an Iowa state
record gar had cleared the brown slurry

of the Raccoon, then splashed home, stirring ripples
that stilled that sulfur scented night.

Dead, Lonnie Wins

For weeks after he's trailered off the dock with heart
failure, lousy cards, and alimony payments always

overdue, his buddies punch his time card and deal
an extra hand for pitch with pots of silver

dimes and quarters Lonnie wins more
often than before. They get how easy it is to lose

your way in December's grime when fingertips
split into bloodless fissures, while river ice

on the Raccoon buckles, and the sun's unstable
light vanishes into yellow chunks behind

the soybean processing plant. In empty
bays when the semis pull away for midnight

runs to Algona, Spencer, and What Cheer, the night
leaks in like a commotion of birds chattering

in maimed cottonwoods. I survived Iowa Parcel
counting minutes until the next belt jam

tossed windshields and transmissions into the stalled
silence, and the black purr of crickets returned

to that parking lot where I waited for my life
to restart, for a replacement dream to arrive.

Late Shift On The Loading Dock

When the power fails, and night locks us
in her arms, our idle words fall
silent as sinners bearing
their souls to the gray planks of a chapel floor;
cicadas swell, a whole
damn orchestra in the stunned
elms outside the gate. I swear
I can hear the cathode ray hum
of the neon go-go dancer on the marquee
at Lola's, half a block away.
Through a hole in the world
where a semi's just pulled out,
she tosses something filmy and bright
into the mangled woodwinds
of crickets and bullfrogs in the swollen
trenches of rain, as eighty dock
workers wait for the power to return,
for parcels to fill the void.

Before We Were Men

I.

Boilermaker, beer back, 2 a.m when I raise my phone
from darkness—number blocked, but I know

the voice, even weeks past the grave. Pre-meth,
scrubbed of manic rambles, the end of each sentence

cracking like a clean nine ball break, *John, dumb fucker,
you never listened to anyone.* No reply,

glasses smack the bar, small gasps from others
like fish dragged on a stringer through Lake

of the Woods. I've heard this story—senior class
president, John raided the graduation fund.

Maybe he's telling an old girlfriend, who's waited
a lifetime, the grand finale. Then he's gone,

just white static hiss of the console TV left on
all night in his parent's basement. As I start to hang up

for good, a bar band bungles the song we sang
for hours of highway miles, hitching home

through November flurries in the Smokies, then
stumbled into day breaking over Lonesome Peak

where John finds the 300 foot drop just in time
to be granted another high, hard 45 years.

II.

In gaps between pickets, I catch John, almost a kid
at dusk, blond hair bobbing above the fence, trying
to snag a peak at life to come. A Zippo

clicks, and the past hovers like a joint passed
hand to hand behind the front desk of The Sleeping Bruin
motel. I hadn't flashed on that place for decades, though

memory, like a mound of cigarette butts
on the boss's desk, smolders behind a padlocked door.
For six weeks I work graveyard shift—peak hours

for lend-lease couples grinding together
like disconsolate rowboats on that stinking river.
In the parking lot, ancient Oldsmobiles, mufflers

strap-tied to cracked frames, write blue exhaust
cloud obituaries. Each night John arrives
at 3 am, from last call at Lola's after-hours

bar, where bail bondsmen gather for seven
card stud. They like him, former all-city power
forward, and don't give a flying

fuck if he wins more than he should. Sooner
or later he'll draw a shitty pair of threes, but refuse
to fold, shaking out pockets for stray bills

while a back corner TV spins black and white test
patterns until dawn. Better to leave clean,
John concludes, casting a last flash of nickels

and dimes into 14th Avenue streetlight, then heads
for The Bruin where someone might swing by
rattling keys to a cherry red future, dragging

motel neon greens and blues through the front door.
Were we happy with nowhere else to go?
At nineteen we hadn't failed at anything.

Last night, I dreamed fingers scrape across
the tin tongue of a mailbox, then reach deep inside,
peeling loose a postcard—fat bear snoozing

on a park bench, an empty picnic basket collapsed
beside, while ZZZZs vanish into an anything's
possible cool night. On the back I find his name,

Room 212, best in The Bruin, and imagine
my old friend lazing through summer heatwave,
before he catches a late night game at Lola's, a full house

of tens and twenties in his hand. When he lets them
go, they flutter free as leaves from a dying elm
outside the green shag lobby before we were men.

Ghost Fish

> *I remember death. And I remember desire.*
> *And they are not the same.*
> —Frank Stanford

The jukebox at Jimmy's sings Hank Williams, George
Jones, Roger Miller, and a single Graham Parson's—

In My Hour of Darkness, which Molly craves
so much she slides half the quarter tips

from Branson tourists into that sweet machine.
After work, she tells me of spring keepers—

tiny fish that feed on darkness, completely
blind. She found them, once, with her brother,

in a cave north of Kimberling City, and she can
find them again. Below the cliff in Goat Holler, she slips

my hand through a crack in the world, rift
in karst, where Permian-age breath's cold

as angle iron. By the time my cheap Sears flashlight
stutters and fades, we've crawled too far to turn

back. She flicks hers off and darkness enters, empties
me of lumen collected in the body.

You promised to be brave, she reminds me, handing
over binders twine, unspooled, and disappears

below a slab of black limestone where I follow
though my shoulders and hips will only fit because

I'm thin as onion skin. Minutes squeezed
below, I'm ready to scrabble back when I hear

her singing *Hickory Wind* and reach out
so she can drag me into a cavern

where her crap light just grazes stalactites
fletching the dome. We whisper across water

of millennia as Molly's beam falls silent
before finding a far shore. And when this freckle-stained

Virgil slips her hand in mine, I'm a young half
baked thing that might never rise, but I can tell

death from desire and squeeze back hard because
soon we'll have to wade into this cold, blind

pool and wait for ripples to still, for the unseen
milk-white creatures to gather.

Postcards from a Massacre

Grandma Ruth, Last Day of School, 1921

Still two hours before first bell on the final day of school
as the ceiling fan stirs a breeze so papers

on Mr. O'Malley's desk rise and walk the aisle,
as if they, too, had someplace better to be.

I'm daydreaming of dancing with Jimmy Dolan when I hear
the tearing sound of old metal wheels rolling down

Cincinnati Avenue and an axle that needs grease.
Even in 1921, when the trolley carries me home each evening

along downtown streets paved for fleets of Ford Roadsters,
the clop of horses' hooves is familiar, though part

of a world we've all outgrown. Now I see Percherons
pounding steel shoes into asphalt that will be slicked

with tar by midday, pulling a buckboard bearing too much
weight on its springs. What's in back, I wonder, stacked

under the heavy tarpaulin? Maybe railroad ties,
or cordwood for the school boiler? On the first of June,

there's a chill in the air, when the sun's still waiting,
and I've got the whole school to myself,

except for steel engraved poets on the wall: Shelley
and Wordsworth peer over my shoulder and Byron

who'd do the Texas Tommy all night long. As the wagon
creeps underneath the window, a finger of light

slides over the Edison Auto Motel and something
sticking out from under the canvas—shoeless feet,

lots of them, some turned up and others down. Manikins
for the windows at Vandevers? But these are black.

And oh lord, now I smell smoke and wonder if the school's
on fire. From this third floor window, I see a dark cloud

on the far side of the railroad tracks—Little Africa.
And later in class, I smell ash and kerosene on Mr. O'Malley's

hands, while he smooths the semester final and whispers
For you, Ruth, as he leans over my desk.

Now students turn to stare as sunlight reveals the death
of Dreamland Theater and a thousand homes rendered

in flame. And I remember the buckboard passing
Central High and turning at McNulty Field, where Babe Ruth

clubbed a baseball so far over the right field wall
it rolled an extra hundred yards to settle by a gravestone

in Oaklawn Cemetery. Now I know where that wagon was bound,
and by tomorrow no one will ever speak of Greenwood again.

Go Down Moses

Mother slipped the cradle into
a cattail thicket behind Brunswick
Billiards, so when she died
the blackbirds called to me
from their nests, a lone male bobbing
on a slender stalk overhead,
chanting: fire, fire, stay away.
When Vernon AME fell
silent after *Be Thou My Vision*,
glass panes shattered: maybe the mob
lobbing stones, or the machine
gun on Standpipe Hill spitting steel
jacketed rounds, or survivors
in the choir loft splitting
the stained glass Sea of Galilee
with World War I rifle stocks,
so they could return
fire. When one last window
remained, the Jesus miracle
of loaves and fishes, flames peered
in empty windows, hugged
the Hotel Stradford, Dreamland,
Red Wing Cafe, then leaped the alley
to Brunswick, where men spilled
into the street waving snapped
cues and rifling the full color
pallet of pool balls into
the white mob. All dead
but Moses, in my basket
below the train tracks where no
one searched, no crosses
burned, no fire could lay claim.

Arron Carter, No Man's Land

While my wife and child drink slurred silence
of sleep and beads of sweat from a cloudless

day have dried, cicadas thread scratched voices,
tree to tree when I pass. Dogs bark their Benedictus

then return to rest as half a moon clears the cloud
litter and Dreamland Theater is stilled. *Blue*

Devils tomorrow, not tonight as the dipper pours
sweet starred life over this green land. Crossing

Latimer, then two blocks down Frankfort Avenue
the last train cars idle, a wall of broken Morse

code dividing this world and the other—black,
white, black. I know I will find you crossing no man's

land like some drunk, half dead doughboy
who stumbles from his trench, then can't

return to either side. I wait for the roar, the terrible
vanishing, a plume of viscera and bone,

but no mines here, just miles of keep-out track—
the Santa Fe and Great Northern Lines and coyote's

shadow as she picks her way between Greenwood
and Tulsa, bearing a fractured squirrel

to her litter, as we returned with rifles our
commanders thought lost in the Forest Arden.

Some nights, murmured words from the other
side—guns glitter in oil drum fire. Are we

ready? Some nights I wait until first light
when maids, porters, gardeners pass over. Only

coyote in the broken coda slides safe between
the stutter of track and shadow, starlight

and shade. I am silence, nighthawk, the grave.

A.J Smitherman, Death of the *Tulsa Star*

I saw him hanging from a streetlamp,
before the fire turned
to ash all the world that remained—
Jack Hardy, centerfield for Tulsa
Black Oilers, gentled his babies
in that scuffed mitt of a left
hand. How will I write
his story, so Clarisa Hardy can cut
him out and post his death
in Wilson's Grocery, so Latisha
Jackson can weep where he fell,
and Clarice Martin scatter a fistful
of chrysanthemum petals
from her window? On the Katy
Line, we're racing north through
Kansas wheat fields, away from
friends stockaded in McNulty
Field. Oh flame of God, oh forsaken
love that breaks over smoking
brick and stone, tomorrow, I will not
wake from all night
type: my last sentence, *These brave
men are gone* will not end
with a bang!
Once I woke and leaned
out the window above my sleeping
press, where 4,000 copies waited
for morning. Red
tracings of aurora had wandered all
the way from Canada, and I believed
even Oklahoma might yet be saved.

Postcard Sonnets from a Massacre

Dear Dreamland,

Smolder of ash, car gutted, smoke ghosted
background for this postcard photograph—one
man felled, nameless, cast loose, dead on the road.
June 1, 1921: Bodies

like cordwood stacked on railcars, forked
in common graves, sunk in mud red waters—lungs
knifed so they couldn't rise. The nothing scraped
from Greenwood streets. Who said you were magic?

One hundred years later, have you risen?
Are you still buried deep? Not the emptied
street, not the old man casting his newspaper
over a broken face. Tell me, Tulsa,

who dragged you here to die? Who wrote you out
of hope while your soul poured into the river?

Citizen
2021

Dear Dick,

Hope poured into the river. Remember
third floor Drexel Building, weary from shoe
shining, you fell against me? I yelled.
The white mob that couldn't lynch you, torched

35 blocks of Greenwood instead. Your
step-mother said you ran for Oregon
fish camp, but I believe sheriff's deputies
seized you hitching for Kansas border, strung

you up—laundry in wings of a dying
cottonwood. Who cut you out, who dragged
your body? Flathead catfish flicker
like damaged light in blood red water.

Come up my love or I will come down, to
sleep with you in the Arkansas River.

Sarah Page
Elevator Operator, Drexel Building
June 15, 1921

Dear Greenwood,

Come sleep in the river we say to those
who remain. Look at this postcard. Ash cloud
halo, flames licking clean the roof we torched
at Vernon AME. No one left

to praise. Can you smell the congregation?
Can you taste human cones of light? From crop
duster Curtiss Hawks, we lob kerosene
bombs—churches, houses burning through the roof,

smoke caressing biplane wings. Below, our
white robes breach Little Africa, pour past
Morse coded dots and dashes of bodies
cast loose sunk deep, never to be claimed.

In the beaten heart of Greenwood, we swear
a thousand bones to silence. Sincerely,

Hyrum Graham
Tulsa Chapter, Ku Klux Klan
June 17, 1921

Dear Sarah,

Among a thousand bones—Althea Gibbs,
Chance Leonard, Jacob Hall—sworn to silence,
bullhead, catfish, gar rise at dusk from
the river. Double sunk bolts that bound us

to Portland cement can't hold what's ready
to let go. Maybe you lean over me,
whispering, tucking away a few stray
hairs, searching muddy water. My love,

do not look for me here in this river.
I am the night praising Tulsa Star, Dixie
Theater, Red Wing Cafe, streetlights huffing
incandescent flame. Lovers unbroken

in the Stradford Hotel, remember me.
I am truth, hope, Dreamland dragged away.

Dick Rowland
Shoeshine Man
June 15, 1921

Dear Greenwood,

For hope, for truth, for Dreamland dragged away,
last quarter notes of a Chopin nocturne—
our Greenwood pastoral—swell then fade.
Moonlight through grated windows freckles

Kimmy's hands on abandoned keys. Safe
inside this Convention Hall, one of hundreds
in this internment camp, Kimmy drives
her bitten nails into white, black notes.

Her fingers remember—allegro,
agitato, reclaiming our magic
city: Mt. Zion, Vernon AME,
Tulsa Star, a thousand homes torn away,

doloroso, grave. Through night sorrow, through
silence, Kimmy's hands fall. La fine?

Latisha Jackson
Reporter, *Tulsa Star*
June 2, 1921

Dear Tulsa,

As silent bodies fall through smoke drifting
down Main, I write *Chess Tournament Just Like Race
Riot*. A single shot. *Enfield,* bolt action
says Judge Bryce who will not leave the game.

We've played through worse: drunk roustabouts tossed
like bricks through plate glass at Madame Fontaine's,
Wobblies, tarred and feathered, hitching a fence
rail home, trolley car rolling down Boston

Avenue, aflame. More shots, we stand,
but the judge waves us back, reads my column,
late afternoon edition, *Nab Negro
for Attacking Girl in Elevator,*

then turns to watch the Right Reverend Jimmy
Flynn drag the last black knight off the board.

Charlie Kramer
Reporter, *Tulsa Tribune*
June 1, 1921

Dear Greenwood,

Dragged from a black silenced night, my boys say
A scout is loyal. They cross the tracks, Frisco
and Santa Fe Rail, from homes in Tulsa
to Greenwood, a dreamland city of brick

and stone, now twisted to ribbons of live
coal. Every diner, doctor's office, theater
ground to clay, *a scout is brave.* Silent, scarves
over mouths pulled tight, they listen for choked

whispers lifting from choir loft risers, for
coughs like penny nails ripped from bone. *A scout
is kind.* Beneath train trestle, from under
cattails unburned, a redwing blackbird startles.

From mud caked wallow, they raise a Moses
Basket of ash. Inside, Greenwood's youngest son.

F. E. Bossard
Scoutmaster, Troop 1
June 2, 1921

Dear Greenwood,

Alone, youngest son stares down a concourse
of potato salad gobbed on his plate.
Released to late May firecrackers miles
away, youngest son rolls on the lawn with

a neighborhood Tom, rakes fingers through lightning
bugs, wheedles mockingbirds gone silent
in shade of Greenwood oaks and ash, tastes
danger crawling over Telegraph Hill.

No skyrockets, no Georgia crackers,
gunshots—youngest son knows family must be
saved. Though no one will listen, he bounds inside,
heart kettle drum banging through his shoes. Youngest

son swallows, tries again, shrieks so loud even
McNulty Park outfield fans turn to hear.

Sarah Carlson
Surviving Sister
May 31, 1921

Dear Greenwood,

Chalk lines blur in McNulty Park outfield—bodies
so thick no pop fly could sink to green.
This evening a north breeze bears a fist
of clouds. In north and southwest baseball stands,

state militia, with long rifles polish
desires, ache to clear the field. Mockingbird
atop the third base foul pole calls *with you,
with you, with you* Mazie, shot dead as we

raced from Dreamland. And where is my Moses
cattail boy she hid beneath a railroad
bridge? Only last week, Jack Hardy hammered
a slow curve, and the crowd levitated

as the ball rode clear to Oaklawn Cemetery,
where bodies burn black by oil fire light.

Aaron Carter
Survivor
June 3, 1921

Dear Greenwood,

Oil blackened bodies—roughnecks, roustabouts,
toolpushers, each night we drag home from rigs,
though stalled hearts stutter to life at dawn. What

god would condemn men to delirium
tremens, flea infected dreams, then, Sunday,
save them for Monday morning Glenn Pool Fields.

Gas pockets ignite, wildcat flames leap two
hundred feet. Evening, imagine, we ride
death's buckboard home with seared corpses, past

Dreamland trumpet and sax jazz solos.
Maybe we could have born this suffering
alone. But fingers busted, knuckles taped

back together, I rise from the wagon
as newsboys cry *Lynch Negro Tonight*.

Carl Weathers
Field Manager, Gypsy Oil Company
May 31, 1921

Dear Dreamland,

Lynch negro tonight, newsboys cry—mass graves,
bullet riddled trees, ash laden breeze.
Beyond the busted road of brick and smoking
flagstone, where the moon wades, a lone redwing

rides a cattail, guards a sleeping child.
I survived, my parents died. This Sunday
morning, *Down by the River Side* leaks through
church plaster and lath. Splash of rain, blue spray

of childrens' laughter slides through buildings
on Archer, Elgin, Martin Luther King
where once boarded stores have been reclaimed:
galleries, restaurants, Greenwood Rising,

Black Wall Street Times. One hundred years later,
in my dreamland, living and dead mount Zion.

Moses Carter
Survivor
2021

Dear Magic City,

From Zion, living and dead were dragged away,
one house, one busted life at a time. Only
concrete stairs remain—no Jacob's ladder
to carry us. Fifty years after, we

still burn. Great grandparents rebuilt, others,
lost, returned from Kansas City, Little Rock,
St. Louis wherever they had flown. Look
at us now—storefronts busted, glass grimed

with neglect, urban renewal slicing
a new white way through Black Wall Street. Just cool
memory in deep August heat— Greenwood,
Oklahoma. No one left to pray that

name. Gutted by fire, scattered like ash,
ghosted by smoke, we, the Dreamland, remain.

Royce Carter
Booker T. Washington High School Graduation
May 31, 1972

The Way to Zion

The summer our church traded us
for a black family from Greenwood,
I was 14, the age of my students
who search these sidewalks for names
of the lost, dead flowers healed
in cold cement. Today, a young
minister waves us inside
her church and leads us upstairs
to a second floor sanctuary, where 100
years ago men and women fell
through smoke from a burning roof
as a biplane strafed the streets, the pilot
tossing kerosene bombs over wings.
I find my pew halfway
back, murmur forgotten names,
and remember my mother, a white
gladiola in a sea of purple
asters and orange trumpet
vine. We rose and sang *When I was
in Egypt land, let my people go.*
Now, as then, we fly
our words over a windrow of ancient
oaks that caught machine gun
rounds and buried bullets
in their sides. Each Sunday morning,
these trees lean close
for hymns spilling across
the street where a baseball game's
already underway, where Moses
Carter in his aluminum folding
chair stationed outside
the barbershop drifts to organ
chords that mingle with blackbird
cries, with the torn open
roar of a crowd leaping
to its feet, like a blue wave
carried through the streets,
all the way to Zion.

… This Time You're Going to Win

Father with Railroad Trestle, 1947

Smoke, steam really, a gray cartoon bubble
blown through oaks over a twilit train
that slows to carry the curve where a trestle fords this

mudsuck of a river—shallows, sandbar, sixty feet below.
1942 Indian Chief, war salvage motorcycle, busted
fuel gauge, abandoned in a field of winter

wheat. After track practice, gunning the engine with left
hand throttle straight up the gravel path
to the top of Lookout Mountain where the whole god

damn city stretched out below: on the far bank,
Julie Rutkowski searches the dance floor at Cain's
Ballroom as Jack Guthrie sings *Oakie Boogie* half

a mile away. When your cycle coughs and dies,
there's only one way back to this first
love. Halfway across the bridge, the steam

locomotive clears the trees, rounds the corner,
cow catcher iron grate V—vacate, valediction,
victim, the whistle blast, a dirge for all dumb

dead things flung over the side. Three
seconds to discover how to survive. For the first
time you know you can die, that bridge shaking

with regret as you fling yourself and twist
in empty space, catch a single railroad tie, fingers
locked as you swing under, the 5,000 ton

Union Pacific angel of death's silvered
wheels, showering sparks. Boxcars raining
soot, your leg kicks out to catch a diagonal

brace. When tracks still, I retell this story you first
shared fifty years before. Morning surfaces
from a dream driven deep as an iron spike, steel

on steel moan of brakes that may never
catch hold. You wipe a hand across smudged light
sifting between railroad ties, then clambor back

into a life worth bearing as a golden eagle,
talons locked on something shaken loose
from the river, rises. Are you listening?

Ghost of Hank Williams at Cain's Ballroom, 1954

An old sock ducked in kerosene burns cheap
and white hot as a human torch scorching

the stage. When lovers catch fire
like moths, the sizzle of wings lights the whole

gray world of loading docks at Mathews Glass
and Meadow Gold where big diesels have pulled

away. Bay doors dragged open, everyone's
listening in—the night clerk at Hotel Fox, firemen

awaiting something more worthy to burn,
winos scraping half-empty bottles

over the parking lot, keeping time. This is one
Friday night and one juke joint on the blue line

south to Red Fork where Charlie Taylor, ground down
to glass, broke and shattered when he fell

80 feet to the drill rig floor. No one
remembers him. No one leads him

out on the dance floor. No one tucks
her small pale fingers in his when even the ceiling

fans can't brush back the high heat of July.
No one leans in and wraps her arms around

his back, or whispers in his ear *I'm So Lonesome
I Could Cry*. Burn me down, thinks Hank,

a stagger of light, a conjunction of shadows,
as he listens from iron steps leading

down to the side bar. Something else is missing—
he pats his shirt for a smoke, feeling vacant:

no more songs waiting for release, no desire
topped off with Johnnie and morphine.

The band stumbles through one last number
before he drifts away into the night.

The Sex Pistols at Cain's, 1978

Sid can see ghosts clinging
to the eaves in this old dance hall, still

shaking on a Saturday night—where else
would they spill eternity, one shot glass

at a time? There's a hole in the wall
of the green room, with its sandbar

of butts and brown smoke stains
leaking through cracks

in the ceiling, where Sid Vicious,
wrecked on smack, punched out

a ragged chunk of plaster and lath.
Now all would-be rockers, waiting

turns for the stage, measure their own
hands, trying to make them fit

the light of that acetylene flame.
On a night that still feels young,

they wonder how one tiny fist
could bear such pain.

Last Texas Playboys at Cain's, 1984

> *My old mistress promised me*
> *that when she died she'd set me free.*
> —Bob Wills

Bob's stopped believing in cornet
valves pressing smoky tunes, in three fingers

of longing scratched on a cocktail
napkin behind an Amarillo bar. All those

nights, with a horsehair bow, conducting
dance hall drunks leaning into *Faded Love,*

but now river maples just shed sadness
over the sidewalk at 2 a.m. Inside

Cain's Ballroom, the last Texas Playboys flap
calcified wings, like cicadas scraping cheap

fiddles, while yellow night lanterned trolleys
totter down Main. Bob fumbles for a nickel,

hoping finally to ride, finds only lyrics
to *Ida Red* while the band grinds away—

dobro and pedal steel lost in time, drumsticks
searching for a high hat weary as mid-July.

Take Me Back to Tulsa, he hums, as the streetcar
tumbles past. Bob stretches his arms

to the sidewalk caterwaul and two steps
home to a western swing pauper's grave.

Taxi Dancer—Cain's Dance Academy, 1932

Creak of tongue
and groove, tuck
of wind, rain presses
bruised palms to the door
at Cain's Dance
Academy where oil
smeared hands once cupped
her back—Ginny, who
stroked my cracked ribs,
and would not spill
through busted knuckles,
while Scott Joplin's *Please
Say You Will* bound us to smoky
light—cigarettes, stale
beer, and susurrations
our feet carved
through cornstarch offerings
dusting the floor. One
nickel, five minutes until
the angel of our bodies
would break again.

Hank's Back, 1961

This last time, he's propped on a stump in a yellow cone
of light and cigarette smoke, as bats, cleaning

the air of midges and mayflies, pass right through.
Maybe Hank believes no one remembers

October of '52 when he collapsed
before the second show. We stood in silence

until we heard soft snores, then slowly filed out—
someone singing under her breath

I Saw the Light. The dead know
they can only catch a couple verses of their lives

stumbling from some honky-tonk. Maybe
that's why he keeps coming back,

tucked in shadows. Not even ghosts can sleep
in Tulsa in mid-July. Tonight something's burning

straight through the hard-baked dirt
outside Cain's though no one seems to notice;

from the side door, we can just see the stage where
the band's playing *Hey Good Lookin'*

badly, and maybe if I'm very still
he'll stick around for the whole damn song.

Ghost

Sometimes in the woods, my dog halts, one foot
raised as if he had rubbed his big wet nose
across the surface of another world,
the same way he listens in sometimes from
the back porch while my wife and I whisper
in the half light of the kitchen. But there's
nothing, just wind hectoring the trees
still clutching leaves they've failed to release,
as near the end, Grandmother held a little
tuck of sheet between her small knotted hands.
It's okay I want to say to my dog,
to the trees, to the ghost, here in this place
of light and shadow. It's okay—in this
common world no one's ready to let go.

At the Red Formica Table Where We Forget
for Dawn

Behind the counter, you slice corned beef
and crack another case of Bud, bottle

caps ringing like shell casings on the counter,
while endless cigarette ash from WWII shell

shocked stutters and falls. All morning their smoke
rises like ice crystals ascending at dawn

when they woke to find one more day returned
to the winter forest where trees split open

and frozen branches cracked and fell,
as if the world, too, were reconciled

to annulment, to life without life, a valley
where men were reduced to small erasures,

staggering, falling in the impossible white
penance of snow. I can hear their syncopated

breathing, church regular, grandmother would have
said, in the silence they compose to slip

the bitter frost of memory that even here,
sixty years removed from the Battle

of the Bulge, leaks under great coats as they gather
in smudged winter light. Sometimes they wake

to luminous nightmares of tracer rounds
and phosphorus shells splintering the darkness

then rise and shuffle together the three blocks
from the VA through slush that has thickened

and refrozen overnight waiting out the hour
before you, too, will rise and return to unlock

the cold metal fragments of memories
they bear so slowly, ill-fitted to the ritual

of living. Envoy from the world beyond, they wait
for you, fixed and polar, star of their firmament

in the neon light of Beggar's Banquet at dawn.

Running the Murder of Pigs Marathon

Slops time late autumn, borderland between
death and dinner on Henderson's farm.

Gray garbage spills over the trough as
400 Hampshires, Durocs, China Whites, the size

of oil drum grills at the VA, where Jerry
H. hoists his beer with three remaining

fingers, chorus snort the boiled pink question
of pig. After eight hours slapping fresh

paint, like cheap lipstick, on a weary
house, I've still got ten training miles to run

down Orilla Road, Henderson's slaughter
shed 30 strides west of the hog lot's hardly

the plains of Marathon, but even Pheidippides,
halfway to Athens, would clap a hand

over nose and mouth gagging past the wire
fence. They're glop-smeared, grinning,

as I wobble, sprinting past without
inhaling. When a baseball bat beaten pickup veers

off blacktop and my sneaker slips
off a steep ravine, the pig mob perks up,

wondering, can we drag him under
the fence. Half a mile later, I slow

to catch a breath in the shade of the only
tree for miles—a crippled cottonwood. *Don't*

look back, I say, but the oink shrieks
of barrows, boars, sows, wet planks tearing,

sound like the pig latin, semi-secret lingo
of my pre-teens. *See you soon,* they squeal.

I yell: *uckfay ouyay igspay.*

At the Track, Waiting for Jesus

Late July, soggy nights, we lean on the rail
for the pre-race parade. My daughter's watching

Don'tmakemelate, a big sorrel that bobs his head
and glares at his rider, as if he wants to spit

out the bit and scream I know which way to go,
while I sneak a few more pages of *Franny and Zooey*

and try to find Jesus in the thousands parked
in their rain rusted seats at the ass end

of another workday. We're blessed with the sacrament
of corn dogs and Buds, boxing quinellas

at a claiming race for quarter horse nags.
Dad, you're not betting, says Laurel, up a couple bucks

and feeling her oats; she shoves a racing form inside
my book and turns back to the rail where horses shy

and skitter. *Okie Dokie,* she laughs,
as the P.A. calls number four, and someone squirts

a pull of Redman at my feet—an ancient jockey
in pink silks grinning down, singing

Dropkick Me Jesus through the Goalposts.
of Life, my favorite song from third grade bible camp.

Two fingers of warm beer in my cup, I dash
for the betting window because who am I to refuse

the muse or Krishna or some blue horse from the caves
of Chauvet, or whoever I've been praying to

for a little saintly advice. Twenty to win
on number four I tell the old gal who laughs

and almost doesn't take the bet but does.
The bell rings, the horses clear the gates,

and my daughter rises from her seat as clods
of mud sail through murky light.

The announcer's calling the final stretch—
Don'tmakemelate in the lead, with Misty's Sister

tucked in along the rail. Don'tmakemelate,
Misty's Sister. In a final photoflash of pixilated beer cans

hurled like Hail Marys, the little whip tail gray
slides past the leggy sorrel beauties.

Okie Dokie, I yell as Laurel tosses her betting slip,
a simple sweet wish that falls

like a petal to the brown lump of tobacco gobbed
on my shoe. *Thank you, Jesus.*

Advent With Audubon

This morning we wake to a barred
owl hooting from the river maple outside
our bedroom window, while Laurel dreams
a grand cotillion of sandhill cranes,
and Nick's migrations through precincts
of dawn flicker with lark and nightingale.
In an hour, Gabe, too, will surrender
to a pintail of light, nightly squabbles over
homework and bedtimes vanished
like the finches and martins we fed thistle
and suet all fall. There's an arctic tern
in the brittle wind as a single jay
on the back porch leaps to the parapet
of ping pong table where a rabble
of squirrels has scattered black sunflower
seeds. It's poetry, practical
as our Audubon Advent Calendar,
that carries me through mornings from here
to Christmas—those small immaculate
doors unseal an aviary of flown winters,
a field guide from accipiter gentilis
to zenaidura macroura. Isn't that what I want,
a prairie warbler to redstart my morning,
a curlew of memory that recalls
me from the gaggle of last night,
when I seemed hell bent on adding one
more grouse to my life list of regrets.
Each morning, our children flock
to the breakfast table to scuffle
for the door where the last passenger
pigeon rises from a lost avian
arcana to a ruby-throated world.

The Deluge

After thirty-four days of rain we wake
to mallards navigating the back lawn
and four survivor squirrels beached
on Gabe's old pitching mound
as a little Niagara breaches the flotsam
of maple seeds clogging the gutter.
In the garage, Nick collects stink bait
and treble hooks, while my mother calls
from two miles downstream to share
her recipe for the end of days—a dash
of sacrifice, a quart of tribulation. Across
the street, neighbors hoist jon boats
and Evinrudes from their garage and lob
a flotilla of empty Budweiser cans
from atop a half-submerged RV.
While a single shaft of light breaks
from a crease in the clouds, neighborhood
cats and dogs gather
on our porch, ranked two by two, just
as my sons' lost turtles return
from months wandering the wilderness.
I wonder how we're all going to fit
in the yellow rubber dinghy Gabe
has launched from his bedroom window.

Honest to God

As I release Laurel and reach for my empty chair,
Gabe and Nick are yawning, rumpled poets

who've slept all night in their metaphors or maybe
just these black suits. I hope they're not

winking at the convoy of bridesmaids already
distracted by mayflies circumnavigating my daughter.

God, I'm glad we're not in church where,
long ago, Nick scattered telltale crumbs from communion

wafers, and Gabe rolled in the aisles, an acolyte
to joy in the port of penitential prayer, while

Laurel weighed anchor, tacking far
from brotherland, past channel isles of hymnals

and the cape of life sucks, until she beached
at the far edge of the world beside Maxine Bosporus

and her pink shoal of used tissues wedged between
three leaky sons. Below us in the half-light

of early evening, someone dances on the mudflats
where fog rises from the Arkansas, as a paddle wheel

slaps pilings under the 21st Street Bridge. I know
this isn't the place, but I want to kiss my wife

on the neck until she laughs and stops crying,
but now Laurel's turning and giving me a little jerk

of her thumb. I'm thinking, oh shit she knows
I wasn't paying attention, and why does the best man

look like Little Billy Bosporus? Nick leans over, pats
my shoulder, and says *You're up, Pops*, and I remember

a whole schooner of used Kleenex has passed under
the bridge since then. I dab both eyes, blow my nose,

pat my chest, wondering who stole my hanky and the poem
I'd stowed in some secret pocket, somewhere.

Stigmata

I grab the morning paper and wave to my 85 year old
neighbor. *Going to be hot,* I say, but Dub's

already there, shirt peeled loose to reveal a smear
of blue tats as inscrutable as cuneiform.

On his front porch, he digs through a styrofoam
cooler and raises a beer as his teacup poodle,

Little Bastard, charges a squirrel that laughs
and slides behind the big oak, while neighborhood

kids cycling the sidewalk, squeal, and try not
to squash the tiny furor now collapsed at their feet.

Dub, too, seems resigned to what he's lost—widows,
who stroll on the far side of the street,

as if he might still bear some nascent power
in that shrunken chest. Perhaps he regrets the names

he bears, the stigmata of Stella, Maggie,
Constance, Leah, Marie engraved in blue, then later

excised in red, as if the heat of new desire canceled
all the old heart thumping epigraphs

to love. Mrs. Haskell and Mrs. Montgomery,
out for their morning stroll, glance over at Dub, coyly,

and wave. Are these the same tattoos they remember:
some scaled blue thing, maybe a mermaid flopped

over one shoulder, a whale and squid on his back
now locked in one gob of tentacles and fins? Lifetimes

later, maybe they're still waiting to see their names
inked in the skin of someone so sad to see them go.

Eschatology

Neighborhood dogs bark a chain letter
chorus, blocks away, that rolls through
backyards down and up each street,
a canine Ponzi scheme of barks,
yips, and howls that call down squirrels
from cottonwood trees. Maybe those
doggy noses smell zip-locked hot dogs
loosed from Mr. Wagoner's cooler,
and floppy ears perk to moonlight scuffling
through bones of antelope, mule
deer, and buffalo that once kicked up
great gobbets of prairie and chewed
through a thousand bluestem meadows.
In the absolute silence of a late
Wednesday, church night, when Taylors
and Turners speak in tongues
of something that once abided here,
the dead return to stir the beacons
strobing red in Frodo, Ajax, and Murphy's
sleep. Woofing, they share their
gladness, this second coming
with every other dumb beast on earth.

Noodling the Void
for Jane

Turn at the skulls on the junkyard fence
says the ancient Cherokee walking the Tahlequah

bridge. As I check the map for Martin's Canoe
Rental, my students rock the bus side

to side, the river calling from far below. After
five more miles of prairie grassland and auto

graveyards, we find them—giant catfish heads,
jaws wide, bearing fathoms of emptiness.

My students wrap silence around slender
fingers, leaning from windows and imagine

floating the gentle current where these monsters
peer up between toes. But they are fourteen

and fear cannot long exclude joy. Out
of the bus, they pass hands through calcified

jaws of beasts, as if to shove their fists
and arms down the vast gullet of some

preternatural terror, to grab it by the guts
and pull free, changed for good.

Dante Gabriel Rossetti's *Beata Beatrix*

When the air clears and the moon returns,
it's *Beata Beatrix* I recall though
Pre-Raphaelite symbolism seems a little
smeary and sentimental for an Okie
on a back porch mulling obsession
and half a bottle of Lone Star. Tonight,
I can imagine Rossetti's suffering:
Lizzie Siddhal dead, how he buried
a reef of new poems clutched
in her pale fingers, then, years later, weary
of scavenging empty creeks
of his imagination for some great mudcat
of a sonnet that didn't want to be dragged
out of its hollow log, he dug her up
at midnight from Christ's Church
Graveyard and found a fat worm
had bored a hole through every page.
If this were Oaklawn Cemetery,
where specters of long dead Okies drag
tired wings through eroded stones,
the ghosts of my cousins, Chris, Matt,
and my uncle John still longing
for something with wheels
would have raised long-necks then
laughed because in Oklahoma
you've got to have a sense of humor
to carry you past the grave.
After that, Rossetti kept painting this one
picture over and over: small details
shifting, a white dove dipped
in cadmium red, the light clearing,
and even Dante in the background
looking up as if to say *what the hell?*

John Everett Millais' Ophelia

Wind stirred branches beat the windows, as a storm
pours over the gutters that have given

up like Hamlet who couldn't even save
his love from drowning. Asters

wave their red wands in the current, Nile
lilies gasp, going under. I dream

of Lizzie Siddal in a two story walk-up where
John Everett Millais has dressed her in a pool

with deep cut banks, her auburn hair pulled
free. A little thunder, a zipper of lightning

scoring the post oak in the front yard carries me
to a London afternoon when I stopped to visit

Lizzie at the Tate while my friends wandered
off to sketch friezes and nudes. After

forty years, what have I forgotten of Millais'
Ophelia: phlox, delphinium, a blue

stream that just fit her body, water lilies bearing
her lightly in their arms? Once,

in another electric storm, lightning cracked
behind the second story farmhouse window where

my wife's hair rose in the surge and all
the lights blew. In the stillness we could hear the guzzle

of bright cold water pouring off
the roof as the wind dredged deep channels

through galleries of corn, leaves bent and turning
palms up in the current, while lancets

of rain furrowed the field. I slipped into
a dream of floating in the moonlight miracle

of earth turned to water. Even here in Oklahoma one
life might be exchanged for another.

Mother at Seventeen

The sky barely lightens. Tiny bats weave
trails of darkness through gaps in oak
limbs stretching over the porch, as if
to protect someone sleeping in a room
upstairs who died years ago. From this porch.
Marilyn hears everything: her father's clotted
snores crawling over the window sill,
sunflowers, blind-eyed, tracking
the light. In this small house, her brother,
sisters savage second hand furniture, and
even the bedroom lock can't turn away
chaos leaking through vents, stretching
two, three fingers at a time
through a gap under the door. She can't
wait to leave. It's a cool September morning
in 1948, when she turns and walks
the half mile to her final year in school.
She hopes someone will finally notice—
the damp flicker of meaning, the brush
of lipstick so subtle only Marilyn knows
she will never return. Beautiful, she knows
grown men would drag her inside
busted lives. What lesson will she haul
through this morning that will not
clear, that will never protect her?
She's watched her father set a hook
in the eye of a minnow he'd scooped
from his tin pail, and she too would
drive her hook through optic nerve,
then drag it back all the way down
the spine if she were able, if she were
not so afraid. I don't blame her anymore.

Pennies

There's little left: narrow chest, air dragged through
a thicket of twigs, furred remains, totem
of small animal bones scraped clean, as if
a cardinal had nested there while he slept.

A lifetime of words have worn deep gullies
where little rain now washes clear. My father
saves the few left. At night he dreams language
passed hand to hand, like binders twine braided

into rope. I wish him memories, whetstone
ground to pure light. I wish him mornings washed
of regret like pennies flushed from a storm drain.
He picks them up, newly reminted, cool

as a mute common tongue, squeezes rheumy
eyes closed, wonders how best to let them go.

Oklahoma Odyssey

Ice slicks Ithaca Street Bridge the late
afternoon I follow five car lengths

behind Grandpa, wondering will he ever
find his way? Driving by dead

reckoning, he swerves to miss every monster
truck, stalled car, raking curb feelers

across bumpers, sidewalls. A tail
light's broken, one shock sprung

so the rear end, like a drunk grasping
for the bar rail, lists after a wide

right turn. No mechanic, I hear the stutter
of seven cylinders. Trojan

red war paint on the quarter panel,
bored into the bumper, a battle flag

of Mycenaean green. Dome light
strobing, I watch the back of his head

as if a film strip were ready to snap loose
from the reel. What we become—tough

fibered muscle and brittle bone.
That's how I remember him, my left

elbow propped on the edge of 1985.
I wave away thirty-five years, the still

massive body that once cut down every
running back rival who crossed

the line of scrimmage, refusing to toss
in the keys. Full moon centered

in late puddles he never misses. I feel
the spray from that night as hope

lingers. Is he still there? Does he
see me a few car lengths behind?

Falling

The year the B-47 Stratojet falls, my uncle's driving
home after losing the heavyweight wrestling

championship and flunking out of Colorado School
of Mines. A bomber his dad built at the mile-long

Douglas plant, Dick watches the wings detach,
engines drop a mile off, and one 18 foot propeller

blade slice straight through a house, the whole family
scattered inside. A Houdini trick, everyone

saved. The pilot pops open a white puff
of cloud in the wreckage of sky, and Dick jumps

out to help this man—snagged in a cottonwood—
return to earth. Miles from home, waiting

until his father's asleep, he's reading Hart Crane's
The Bridge, hauled through wrestling rooms

from Fort Collins to Albuquerque and now endless
Oklahoma grasslands. While water, from a jerry

can he's poured on the old Ford's block, transmigrates
to steam, Dick watches wind part winter wheat,

an ocean liner slicing the heartland.
When he tries to conjure the bridge, Dick can't

get past the story of Crane on the stern
of the Orizaba, waving to someone who has turned

to watch. The wind moves on, the furrows seal
over, and he imagines drowning in a vast

Midwestern prairie. I'd like to tell you no one
died when that B-47 tore loose from the sky.

I'd like to tell you my uncle returned to his freshman
year and learned to bear the world gently

in those brutal arms. I'd like to say Crane didn't
despair but stumbled and fell into Gulf chop.

Years later I sat beside my uncle's hospital bed,
though he'd never wake again, and listened

to my aunt retell the story—how Dick lost
the Olympic trials on a single penalty point. *Watch*

the leg sweep, she whispers in his mauled
wrestler's ear. *This time, you're going to win.*

Florence Learns to Fly

What is sixteen? A blown dandelion in Chinook
wind. What are two thousand miles, leaving behind

a mother leaking slow-drip crazy? Florence
rides east from Oregon with only pocket-change for one-

way, four days to Alabama. Outside
Supai, the bus, torn from high desert thirst, staggers

to the gravel shoulder as a bi-winged Curtiss Lark breaks
from the void. She shoves her way off, skirts

flapping over the edge of the earth. When
the pilot, scouting for Warner Brothers, offers

a ride in the front seat, she flies from a dirt-bound
world, then barrel rolls over the south rim

into cumulous bounty, straight through Arizona
cloud banks that hang over the Colorado

dredged from darkness five thousand
feet below. What the hell comes after that? Wheels

chocked, throttle choked down to stall, the lovely
young man hands her back to the bus still

waiting at Texaco, so Florence reenters
her journey—Flagstaff, Arizona to Mobile, Alabama,

where her father, plantation foreman, locks her
in an attic room. She bobs her hair, slides out

a garret window, drops from a walnut tree
leaning over the roof to dance the black bottom

with One-Armed Willie Jackson's Orchestra
on Dauphine, because she can't remain in one

bolted down moment too long. Seventy
plus years later, I hold Grandma's chilled

hand as tiny sips of oxygen thread through
arteries, capillaries, ailerons. Though this was never

a story she whispered, Dad, horizon-gazing
all week, hands me a postcard signed by a movie star

and recalls ragged chunks, as if memory
could only be banged back together one wing

strut, one stuck rudder at a time. She leans
into the prop wash cranking the big Panavision

camera as Howard Hughes parts the lips of the Grand
Canyon, banking hard right as Florence spreads

arms wide to lift this rattling fabric
covered kite of a plane free from the grave.

www.ingramcontent.com/pod-product-compliance
Lightning Source LLC
Chambersburg PA
CBHW020947090426
42736CB00010B/1302